Rockwood

Poems, Prose and Musings

Howard B. Pierson

Order this book online at www.trafford.com
or email orders@trafford.com

Most Trafford titles are also available at major online book retailers.

Note for Librarians: A cataloguing record for this book is available from Library
and Archives Canada at www.collectionscanada.ca/amicus/index-e.html

ISBN: 978-1-4269-0131-7 (soft)
ISBN: 978-1-4269-0133-1 (ebook)

We at Trafford believe that it is the responsibility of us all, as both individuals and corporations, to make choices that are environmentally and socially sound. You, in turn, are supporting this responsible conduct each time you purchase a Trafford book, or make use of our publishing services. To find out how you are helping, please visit www.trafford.com/responsiblepublishing.html

Our mission is to efficiently provide the world's finest, most comprehensive book publishing service, enabling every author to experience success. To find out how to publish your book, your way, and have it available worldwide, visit us online at www.trafford.com

Trafford rev. 6/11/2009

www.trafford.com

North America & international
toll-free: 1 888 232 4444 (USA & Canada)
phone: 250 383 6864 • fax: 250 383 6804 • email: info@trafford.com

The United Kingdom & Europe
phone: +44 (0)1865 487 395 • local rate: 0845 230 9601
facsimile: +44 (0)1865 481 507 • email: info.uk@trafford.com

Angels

My friend - Do you believe in angels?
Well, I believe they are everywhere!
And I believe that God sends an angel,
At times to deliver the answer to prayer.

I believe that we entertain angels,
And most times we don't realize,
That human beings are angels,
And they are placed here by God in disguise.

Now just try to imagine if you can,
That an angel is either a woman or man.
And think of someone that you met in the past,
That did you some kindness that forever will last.

Then just close your eyes - and realize
That an angel has visited you -
Now you can reach out your hand to some
woman or man,
And be an angel that's just passing through.

And oh yes, there are unseen angels
That surround us from time to time,
To protect us from unseen danger
You will hear them if you open your mind.

A Friend

Early in the Bible we read about “His” plan
How “God” created woman and gave her to the man
And there was love

It was there in the garden that love would come alive
And they saw that codepedence would help them both survive
And there was love

Then the serpent came between them and the woman did deceive
Then the woman tempted man that day
And made the man believe
That there was love

God looked upon the work he’d done
And saw that it was great
Then He instructed man and woman to go and procreate
And let the people multiply and spread throughout the world
And they would be His children
Yes every boy and girl
And there would be love

I'm Slowing Down

I'm sixty four years of age and it seems
That all my life I have done everything
As though I was on production

The work had to be finished as soon as possible
If I was going somewhere I must get there early or on time
If I had an appointment I must make it on time
Never be late!
I allowed myself to be pushed and pulled by others

It might be hard to say - I'm not going to finish this today!
If you are in a hurry, you go on ahead!
If I'm not there don't be surprised!
My health nor my speed are not what they used to be.
I'm slowing down.

Just Suppose

Now suppose that the media began to refuse
To report anything that resembled bad news
And suppose that tomorrow on the T.V.
There are nothing but beautiful things to see

Now suppose that all churches merged overnight
And we all came together, both black and white
And suppose that money played no part
In the houses of God - Would that be a good start?

Now suppose that all people felt the need
To share everything and abolish all greed
And suppose that all men and women could say
All things are going to be equal today

Suppose every husband would honor his wife
And the women would stay with their husbands for life
And all the children could truly see
What marriage and family was meant to be

Suppose that educators around the world
Began to let love and laughter unfurl
And politicians began to pray
And speak well of others in every way

And suppose that stress should cease to exist
Could we possibly live in a world like this?

Creely

Nobody liked old Creely
They were glad when he went to his grave
Old Creely was mean and wicked
He would beat his only slave

And they say he was mean to his family
His wife and children as well
Maybe that's why they wrote on his tombstone
"Old Creely is resting in Hell"

All the neighbors hated old Creely
Old Creely was wicked they said
Now his wife and children are better off
Now that old Creely is dead

There were only two men in the county
That would bury old Creely that day
And they did it because of the money
The family had offered to pay

Nobody came to the funeral
There were just Jim and Tom Brown
And they made it easy for Creely
They buried him upside down

Forgiveness

Oh I could hate you for the rest of my life
If I wanted to live that way
But I know this is not in keeping
With the prayer Jesus taught us to pray

Forgive us as we forgive others
I believe this is what Jesus said
And when he spoke of the unbelievers
He referred to them as the dead

So I forgive that I might be forgiven
By the father who liveth in heaven
And I ask his blessings on those I forgive
And to pour out his grace that they too will live

Many mountains are built out of hills of kindness
they say
And I want to build me a mountain to stand on
someday.

I want to look down on this wicked world that I trod
Reach out my hand and touch the hand of God

And to know that I am forgiven

Reflections

Constant reflections on what might have been
Seems a bit ridiculous to me
What if God had reflected on what might have been
When he looked down on us and did see
The mistakes that we'd made and the things we did
wrong
And told us that we should have been strong
"Too late" he would say you committed the sin
There will be no forgiveness - Think of what might
have been
Now reflect on your past for the rest of your life
And remember nothing but trouble and strife
These reflections would hold no future you see
Life would now be empty for you and for me
But he says we're forgiven - its time to move on
Today was tomorrow and yesterday's gone
There is a heavenly future that lies straight ahead
And life everlasting and yesterday's dead

Share

If we should grow old and grow selfish
The selfishness stands in the way
That's why younger people despise older people
Whenever the older turn gray

So I challenge you older people
To share what you have with the young
And I promise you will never regret it
After the last song is sung

The young will enjoy what you have to share
Whether great wisdom or praise
And there will always be some younger person
somewhere
That will help you get through your maze

So give of your heart, your love or your money
Whatever you might have to give
But do not grow old and selfish
You will find that's the hard way to live

Because if we grow old and selfish
The selfishness stands in the way
And the younger despise older people
That are old and selfish and gray

Man and Woman

God took the woman from the man
And gave her back to man again
God wanted things to be this way
When he created woman that day

Now woman draws her strength from man
And then she give it back again
And there is love

If man deserts the woman
And leaves her all alone
Then woman longs for his return
Her source of strength is gone

But if woman leaves the man alone
He has no one his strength to share
He waxes old and mourns his soul
For this he can not bear

Tis good for man and woman
Together then to stay
Because that is how God made us
He wanted it this way

Rescue Me

For too long now my soul has filled with sorrow
While hanging on to hope - that change will come tomorrow

Depression keeps me in despair
I feel her hatred everywhere
And though I pray to God each day
To make this hatred go away

God doesn't seem to hear my prayer
Her hatred lingers in the air
It seems to me there's no escape
I must endure this awful hate

I've searched my soul for reasons why
At times I've wished that I could die
But nothing comes that might explain
Why I must always live in pain

Again, oh God, I come to thee
And ask that Thou would rescue me

Fountain Pen

If you would, lend me a bit of your time
I have a brief story to tell
I grew up using the fountain pen and each desk
Had an ink well
The ink bottle had a small lip inside
That held enough ink for one pen
To fill up the lip you would tip the bottle
Then set it upright again
Not every one used the lip for refilling
But I was one who did
And whenever I used my fountain pen,
It was observed by the other kids
You know that kids will always play pranks
And this day they played it on me
They loosened the lid on my bottle of ink
And then everyone waited to see
I sat down at my desk, piked up my ink
And tilted it far to the right
To fill up the lip, but the cap slipped
And the ink made a terrible site
The other kids laughed and I sat there in pain
And I never used the ink lip again

Friend

Now friend, I'm writing this poem to you
Because frankly, I know it's the right thing to do
As both of our lives grow closer to end
I wanted to thank you for being my friend
I want to thank you for all you have done
The acts of kindness, each little one
The time that you gave me, the thoughts that we shared
The assurance that you always cared
For the times that you listened as I poured out my soul
And for the times when you were down
And you let me take hold
For the wine and the laughter we both had to share
The joy of knowing you would always be there
For the many long hours we talked you and I
Honest and open with never a lie
You understood me and I understood you
That made our friendship all the more true
So I'll just say that I hold our friendship quite high
And it's something I'll cherish till the day that I die

Take Courage

Take courage - take courage, my friend
Take courage - take courage, I say
And courageously stand up for what you believe in
And be honest and do not dismay

With courage walk on through the tumult
And sound your own shofar I say
Go out with a smile and have courage
it will help you to get through the day

Give what you can give to others
And expect not a thing in return
But listen to what they are saying
And ???? the things that you learn

Go out and enjoy the functions
And mingle around with the crowd
But don't give in to lies and repression????
And leave if the noise gets too loud

Take courage, my friend - take courage
And don't ever forget who you are
Listen for God o'er the tumult
And keep sounding your own shofar

Rejected
No Doubt

Friend have you ever been rejected?
That's an awful thing to go through
It makes you feel unwanted
And it make you feel like a fool

My rejection began I guess when I was just a kid
I would wonder if it might have been
Something I'd said or maybe something I did?
I don't think the other kids meant to be mean
Although sometimes I had lots of doubt
It seems that when they would choose up their team
They always left some kid out
And that kid was usually the lonely one
Who the other kids said was not any fun
Well I know how it feels to be left out
And that's how Jesus felt a I haven't a doubt

Your friend

He Touched Us

When your world and my world collided
We both fell off into the sea
And when we emerged to the surface
I was holding you and you were holding me

Your world and my world kept moving
And we looked up to heaven above
God saw us both there just drowning
Drowning in our sea of love

He reached down his hand and he touched us
And brought us both safely to shore
And gave us a new world to live in
To be happy in love forever more

Storms of Life

Into each life a little rain must fall
That's what makes us all grow strong and tall
So if I seem so big and tall and strong
That's because it rained into my life so long

And if I seem so independent brave and free
And if you think you'd like to walk through life with me
There's one thing to consider before you do
When it rains on me it also rains on you

Each bridge we burn together, each hill we cross
Each river each mountain we climb
It's a long long way to the end of the earth
And it won't always be sunshine

Darkness and Light

Friends - we all have a light side and dark side
This pertains to both women and men
And we all try to show the light side
While the dark side stays hidden within.

They say "You can run, but you can not hide!"
And they are referring here to our darkness inside.
So if we can not run and we can not hide,
We must confess the darker side.

This is the way we get it all out
And relieve ourselves of anxiety and doubt.
Now once this is done, there's a vacuum inside
And if we keep the light shining there's nothing to hide.

Now if we let the light shine and guard against sin,
That's when we can begin to let love enter in.
And the spirit of love will bring us true bliss.
Now aren't you glad that I've written you this?

Your friend

God made a triangle of faith, hope and love
That his people might be free from sin

Satan made a triangle of lust, greed and pride
That he might deceived God's people
And make them disbelieve

The Black Bag

That bag just set there on the shelf
Not mine, I kept on telling myself
But the small voice that comes from inside
Said perhaps your ancestors had something to hide

That bag was at least a hundred years old
In our family for over a century I'm told
I remember my father and uncle would say
The truth in that bag will come out someday

For years now I had forced myself to restrain
From looking at something that might bring me pain
But today that little small voice from inside
Was saying "Open it up, you have nothing to hide"
But that bag has been in this family for years
It made mother cry and dad shed a few tears
But the little small voice now becoming a scream
Said that must mean your ancestors did something mean
No! My folks were always good people, I know
I've heard both my mother and father say so!

Then the small voice began to subside
"Oh, well, then you know you have nothing to hide"
Then the voice changed and I heard daddy say
"The truth in that bag will come out someday"

But wait, my dad is long dead and gone
This can be him speaking
Something is wrong!

It was then I remembered my Uncle Ralph
And how when that bag was mentioned
He would rare back and laugh
And I remembered how Daddy would sit and brag
About how proud he was of what's in that bag

And now I was listening to the small voice inside
That said "Open it up, you have nothing to hide

Then I began to feel brave as I took the bag down
This bag that had once been the talk of the town

All the stories I'd heard about the bag
And the time I'd listened to my Daddy brag.

All these feelings came to me ----
And I was compelled to look inside you see
So I closed my eyes and uttered a prayer
That God would help me
With what I found there

Then I opened it slowly
It looked like an old rag
I took it out and unfolded
<u>THE CONFEDERATE FLAG</u>

The Psychologist

It has occurred to me my new found friend,
It's an awesome job that you do.
This might not be your chosen profession,
The profession may have chosen you.

You will always have people coming to you,
On the edge of suicide.
And there will be days my new found friend,
That you will want to run and hide.

Well, you can run but you can not hide.
You can help prevent someones suicide,
And there is something else I might say here as well,
You might have already helped to save this soul from hell.

But be sure that Satan will try to deceive,
So just hold on tight to what you believe.
Remember that God will see you through,
With this awesome job that he gave you to do.

Remember the words that you gave me my friend,
Pray without ceasing right out to the end.

A Friend

Paradise

Let me dream and dream and dream
I've earned this place in life
What ever my mind can imagine
And hope that it comes from God
Along the back roads of my mind
There are always green pastures
Deer and cattle roam together
And drink cool water from the glistening stream
Birds of different feather fly overhead
And the sky is a light shade of blue
The trees are walnut and weeping willow
Growing alongside the stream
A squirrel barks and pops its head around the tree
A plan flies high overhead against the sun
A cardinal and a robin perch side by side
On the rusted barbed wire fence strung
Out on chestnut posts that have faded almost white
The honeybee is taking nectar
From the willow tree and the blue jay
Landed on a rock out in the stream.
No, this isn't paradise. It's only a dream
But that's okay because when I close my
Eyes again to dream, I'm back in paradise again

The Book

Friend I've lived a long time
And I haven't a doubt
That some day soon
This life will run out

But I'm hoping to leave you a little advice
That will help you to make your life turn out real nice.
There is a book that was written, you know
It was written by prophets a long time ago.

The Bible was written to speak to us all
To give us direction in case we should fall.
And I guess we've all fallen from God's grace, so to speak
Because His redemption we all failed to seek.

To recognize Jesus who came here to save
The souls of us all before reaching the grave.
Yes, I've lived a long time but I have no doubt--
That some day soon this life will run out.

Your friend

Pride Gets In The Way

Have you noticed my friends that when you read these poems
That they all seem to have the same ring.
Well that's because when God gave me this talent,
He made it a simple thing.

God didn't want one of His servants
To get all excited inside.
He didn't want Howard Pierson
To swell up and burst with pride.

So He said now let's just keep it simple
And this is the way you'll convey
The message I want you to pass on
To your friends
As you write for them day after day

When pride doth surround you
Then evil will come,
And you will grow weak and your spirit
Will numb.

So don't get prideful, it stands in the way
Of the message I give to you to convey.

Your friend

Train of Life

Friend if you were riding on a train
And the conductor should happen by
He might want to look at your ticket
And if you had none, he might want to know why.

He might ask your destination
Or ask where you got on board.
Or he might just glance at your ticket
And leave without saying a word.

But be certain the conductor would ascertain
That you had the credentials to be on the train.
But as he does his job - now your ride is secure.
You will now reach your destination for sure.

Are your credentials in order on the train of life
Just in case the conductor comes by
Is your ticket in order, destination clear
Is there anything in your baggage to fear

Is your luggage filled with contraband
Of which you should dispose
Or does your ticket to ride contain something to hide
Then you will be put off the train I suppose.

Prayer of Thanks

Thank you God
For showing me what I must do
Oh I'll suffer a lot before I am through
But I hope when I'm finished that
I've helped someone to know
That you are calling us home
And someday we must go.

Your friend

It Could Be You

That little gang of ducklings
Were as cute as cute can be.
They were all very pretty and yellow.
Well, that is, all except "Me."
"Me" was another color.
"Me" was as blue as the sea.
And me myself had been blue at times.
So that's why I named him "Me."

Now Mother Duck rejected "Me,"
And she never treated "Me" good.
So one day "Me" just ran away,
Like I always knew "Me" would.
And "Me" somehow wound up down by the lake
Where "Me" happened to meet a friendly old drake.

That old drake looked at "Me" and thought
Well, what is this thing?
Then he reached out and took "Me" under his wing.
Now "Me" had a friend and it filled "Me" with pride--
You see that friend made "Me" feel real good inside.
There is something to learn here I hope you can see--
And if you are asked where you learned it,
Well you learned it from "Me!"

Your friend

Humble Me Lord

I gave her a couple of poems to read
And I watched her frown and wince.
Then she looked up at me and said,
“This stuff just doesn’t make sense!”

Now she’s an intelligent person
And known quite well around town.
Coming from her, that kind of remark
Could have been a tremendous let down.

But I was determined and so I just went on
When I could think of some lines to write
And I would pray for God to give me more words
When I got into bed each night.

And I prayed for acceptance from others
As they would read these poems that I wrote.
That they would not sound too simple or silly
Or somehow be far too remote.

I never did get a clear answer from God
But now I believe I know why.
God wanted me to spread my own wings
And to see just how high I would fly.

It's all too familiar now
And thinks seem so much better somehow.
Something happened yesterday
That turned all your blue skies to gray.
And you didn't sleep much at all last night
But today you realize it's going to be alright.

It's all too familiar now
But things seem a little better somehow
The gray skies are going away
And the sun will shine in today.

It's all going to be okay
No more troubles and no skies of gray
Yes, the sun is going to shine
And things will be fine this time.

It was just a lover's quarrel that made
You feel that way
When love become too familiar
There is always the devil to pay.

It's all to familiar now
But things are so much better somehow
The trouble has all gone away
And time is taking care of today.

It's okay.

Enjoy The Mystery

Friend, here is something I learned that I'll pass on to you.
Don't plan away all your tomorrows whatever you do.
You know tomorrow holds so much mystery!

If we plan away our tomorrows ~ we miss it you see.
So just hold back and see what tomorrow will bring.
It might be a very marvelous thing.

Some people plan their whole life away,
They live in the tomorrow and miss out on today.
Don't rob yourself of what tomorrow might bring.
The "mystery" can be such a marvelous thing.

So enjoy the mystery as long as you live.
This is a gift to yourself you can give.
Be not anxious about the tomorrow I say,
And let tomorrow bring whatever it may.

Your Friend,

Of These Beware

Be careful my friends as you go about town,
I hear there is a ruthless gang hanging around.
And caution the children when they go out to play,
They will encounter this gang almost every day.

One is called "ego" and one is called "greed",
These two always demand so much more than they need.
Then there is one called "power" and another called "lust",
These are two villains you really can't trust.
One is called "anger" and the other is called "hate",
Steer clear of these two before it's too late.

Watch out for this gang they are usually spread out.
But they are heavily armed and they have lots of clout.
They leave lots of hurt and despair in their wake,
So watch out for them all for goodness sake.

They don't stay in one place, they are all on the go,
And sometimes you will meet them and not even know.
Power ~ Ego ~ Hatred ~ Lust and Greed with Anger,
This gang we don't really need.

Your Friend,
Howard Pierson

Poets

Everyone wants to be a poet
But only for a while
A true poet knows the loneliness
But goes the extra mile

When someone writes a poem
With feeling -- so I am told
There's an openness they want to share
That comes from inside the soul

The brightest poems are poems of glee
Something the poet wants all to see
But the darker poems and this I've been
told
Let the reader see the darkness of soul

We all have spirits both dark and light
And the dark spirit holds a containment
of fright
So as the good spirit tries to prevail
The dark spirit hides in its own little hell

You can always tell when the poet is sad
Because the good will be there
But so will the bad

MOUNTAIN DOGWOOD

It seems like only yesterday,
The world was cold, and dark, and gray.
And all around was only death.
Stark and lifeless without breath.

Then in the mountain side suddenly
A glow of heaven there seemed to be
A pure etherally white like trace.
Interwoven like purest lace.

The falling rain like fingers of God.
Wrought miracles in the lifeless sod.
And suddenly most everywhere
Dogwood blossoms filled the air.

Never before in years gone by
Have I seen such glory neath the sky.
I praise Him as I lift my face
Toward heaven in thanks for this glorious lace.

NEW RIVER DOE

With tiny feet moving quietly,
   And head turning to and fro
Eyes looking out for danger,
   My gentle New River doe.

Hide colored brown like the woodland,
   Legs filled with muscle power
Nibbling on fresh green grasses,
   She moves through her Eden-like bower.

Smooth and soft as marshgrass,
   I sigh, as I watch her go
Her head'll hang in a hunter's lodge,
   My gentle New River doe.

ON LEAVING A SUMMER COTTAGE

When days have been clean and memorable,
   For those hours I often grieve.
Times of fun are, finished and gone.
   But its oh so hard, to leave.

When smells are gone from the kitchen,
   And the floor is all, scrubbed and clean.
The front porch is swept and the door is locked,
   I hate to leave the scene.

CREATION

The sculptor with a stone can see,
   That which is hidden from you and me

Slowly, carefully he chips away,
   The outward concealing robe of debris

And then at last there stands revealed,
   That which for eons has been concealed

A figure perfect to suit the eye,
   Which beneath the surface did surely lie

To the eye of an artist who seeks to find,
   In the depth of the stone what he has in mind.

ABANDONED

Dusty moldy hay,
   Clodded dry urinated manure
Torn twisted cow halters
   Irreparable fancy side saddle
All useless to this microchip age

In a barn long since abandoned
   Long since empty of bull bellows
And cattle lowing, horses neighing
   Some thing have lasting worth
And to ship technology tie with binder twine.

SOUNDS

Hungry trout after twilight flies,
   Making cautious ripples in hidden pools
Water slapping gently against pier posts,
   And resting boats quietly replying.

Rain dances on tin barn roofs,
   With overfilled down spouts gushing gaily
The brooks babble as rocks invade its smoothness,
   And high falls scream with downward delight.

Crickets creak their monotonous melody,
   As mockingbirds sing in merry mimmick
Hunting dogs hound the evening moon
   And hens sit nesting sleepily.

Winters crackling wood burning sounds,
   Icicles hang in swaying wind chime rhythm
Snows crispy crackerlike crunching,
   Resounding roadway rut ridges rattle

Sounds of spring, summer, fall and winter,
   Each season endowed with its own
Accompanied by Mr. and his invented,
   Make alive the sounds of life.

YOUR WORD

Don't make a promise you can't keep,
   Stay out of debt or you'll get in deep
Know what you're doin before you say,
   Folks don't want to wait all day.

Man builds his life on his word,
   All folks know is what they've heard
Be very careful with what you do,
   Cause folks soon put judgment on you.

PRIMITIVE

Long stretching ribbons
   of concrete,
Grease, oil, and tire
   skid maimed,
Cutting unkind swaths,
   thru primitive forest,
And barren flat land.

Steepened mountains
   tiny crawling fingers,
Large behemoths belching
   unkind clouds of sickening smoke,
Dribbling tracable oil
   paths intermingled.

Gum wrappers, banana skins
   diminutive debris,
Dancing crazily, seeking refuge
   from manmade whirlwinds,
Flying cars, crying kids, depressed
   Dads, mouthing mothers,
Hot car, cold car, flat tire,
   steaming motor,
Concrete confusion, interstate
   jungle.

TINY BIRD

Teenie tiny flying flitterer,
   You are such a noisy twitterer,
I wish you'd quiet down,
   And sit on your sitterer.

I SEE YOU

In the arms of a winter dead tree,
   That opens blossoms spring white,
In the cry of a tiny creature,
   Shattering a peaceful night.

In the stirring of some tree-hidden nest,
   Or deep grass steeped rabbit burrow,
Or new mown spring fresh hay,
   And fresh turned garden furrow.

I see you God and wonder how man,
   Who came as a personal creation from you,
Can look about as spring starts awakening
   And deny your existence as we do.

TO AN ELUSIVE DEER

Tiny elusive creature,
   How can you come so close,
And I never see you?

How do you so easily blend,
   Into green forest foliage,
And be so near and not hidden.

I see your tiny fresh tracks,
   Breathing new earth punctures,
I am quiet, you are near yet so far.

Someday tiny one we shall meet,
   On some forest path yet untrodden
And I shall know you, though we've never met.

JUST A PONE

Little bit a cornmeal some fresh buttermilk,
   Pour in a fryin pan smoother than silk
Fire up the woodstove use wet rag test,
   Bake until golden brown, reckon is best.

Put on the table still in the pan,
   Fit for a king or a plain workin man
Lots of country butter to melt on top,
   Don't mind the calories eat till you pop.

Nothing better in the country or town,
   I've tried everything, and I been around.
Lookin for the best, let no more be said
   Nothin better than a pone of cornbread.

SPRING WATER

How fondly I remember
   The springhouse on the farm
With its abundant cool water,
   When the day was more than warm.

After the plowing was over,
   And the sun began to set
My throat was dry and scratchy,
   And I longed for something wet.

I had the best of all drinks,
   No matter what one can afford
Cool, clear spring water,
   Drank from an old green gourd.

HOMEMADE BREAD

The woodstove is hot and cracklin,
   The steam clings overhead
The smell of smell entices,
   Ain't nothin like homemade bread

Soon pipin hot from the oven,
   Smells nearly drivin me wild
I lay claim to the heel,
   Cause I'm the oldest child

Smother with fresh country butter,
   Dunk in a glass of cold milk
Nothin could taste any better,
   Goes down smoother than silk

If I could go back to my childhood,
   There's nothin more to be said
Just lead me straight to the kitchen,
   And fill me with homemade bread.

FEET

Have you ever sat in a shopping mall,
   Or on some busy street?
To make an in depth study,
   Of everybody's feet?

Some are fat and ugly,
   Others are neat and trim
A few are tired and beaten,
   While many are filled with vim.

A few are down in the heels,
   And some split at the side.
Many march along so happy,
   Others their hurt try to hide.

I guess the best I"ve ever seen
   Far from the city street
Hopping along a country lane
   A boy with dirty bare feet.

BALLROOM DANCING

Some folks would say I'm old timey,
   Others might call me a square
But bring back the moonlight ballroom,
   And the bands that once played there.

Bands like Woody Herman,
   Or maybe Sammy Kaye
Perhaps a Guy Lombardo,
   And music Duke Ellington's way

Hold your lover tightly,
   To the rhythm softly sway
Maybe some boogie woogie,
   As you toss your partner away

Others would like some waltzing,
   To the music of Lawrence Welk
As you glide the floor with your chosen,
   The melodies smooth as silk.

Call me a square if you want to,
   But I'll go anyway
To some romantic ballroom,
   To hear some big band play.

TINY LEAF

Tiny leaf unfold,
   Let your glory thru,
Your tree needs shelter,
   She depends on you.

The suns warmth beckons,
   Come forth from winter's rut,
Show your spring finery,
   God gave His very best.

Open tiny leaf,
   Fear no longer cold,
Spring is here at last,
   Tiny leaf unfold.

TO A WASP

Devilish tiny creature,
   Disturbing my morning rest.
Buzzing angrily, busily,
   You give my temper a test.

Land where I can reach
   And I shall crush you flat.
Devilish tiny creature
   Buzzing round my hat.

Modern Conveniences

Mama got rid of the Maytag,
   she threw the old thing away
Papa bought a washer and dryer,
   but she still washed once a day.

Next she got rid of the woodstove
   bought an electric and a microwave
When we brought in a stereo,
   Mama became a slave.

With the house completely automated
   she can hardly catch her breath
Just one more modern appliance,
   and we'll work poor Mama to death.

www.ingramcontent.com/pod-product-compliance
Ingram Content Group UK Ltd.
Pitfield, Milton Keynes, MK11 3LW, UK
UKHW061830190726
13855UKWH00005B/1734

9 781426 901317